Learning Is Fun!

KATHY ROSS C·R·A·F·T·S
COLORS

by Kathy Ross

Illustrated by Jan Barger

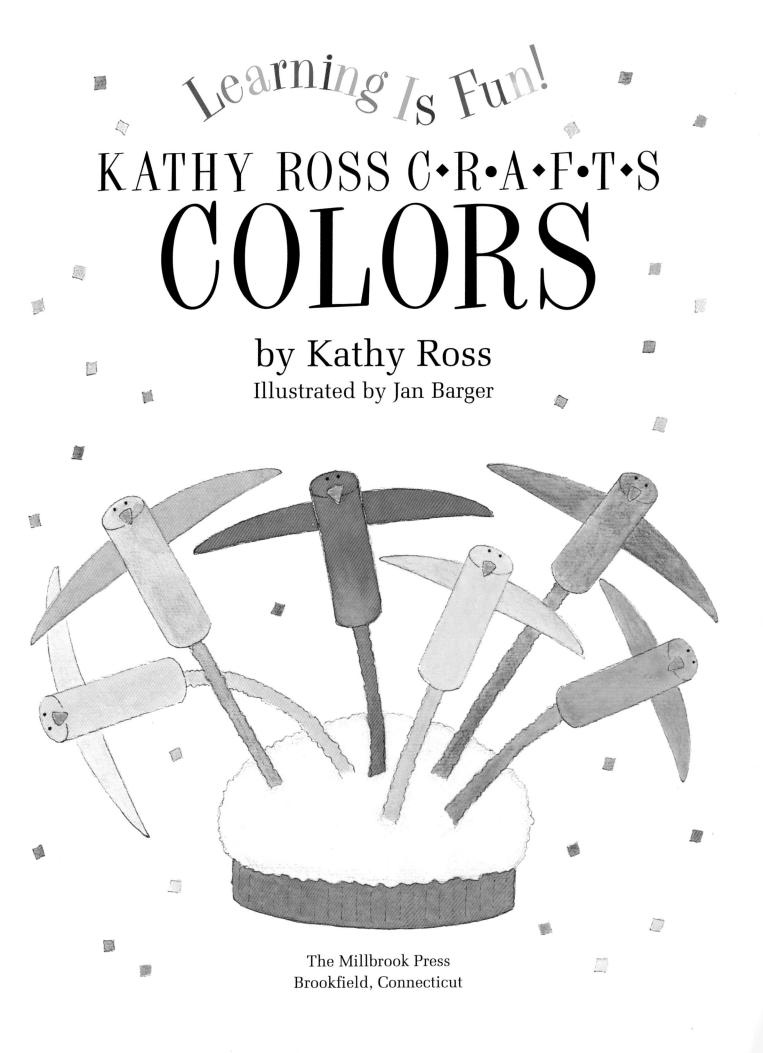

The Millbrook Press
Brookfield, Connecticut

For Julianna Jellybean!

Library of Congress Cataloging-in-Publication Data
Ross, Kathy (Katharine Reynolds), 1948-
Kathy Ross crafts colors / Kathy Ross ; illustrated by Jan Barger.
p. cm. — (Learning is fun!)
Summary: Provides step-by-step instructions for twenty-one simple crafts
intended to teach about colors.
ISBN 0-7613-2651-0 (lib. bdg.) — ISBN 0-7613-1947-6 (pbk.)
1. Handicraft—Juvenile literature. 2. Color—Juvenile literature.
[1. Handicraft. 2. Color.] I. Barger, Jan, 1948- ill. II. Title.
III. Learning is fun! (Brookfield, Conn.)
TT197.5.T65 R67 2003   745.5—dc21   2002152484

Published by The Millbrook Press, Inc.
2 Old New Milford Road
Brookfield, Connecticut 06804
www.millbrookpress.com

Printed in the United States of America
lib: 5 4 3 2 1
pbk: 5 4 3 2 1

Table of Contents

KATHY ROSS C·R·A·F·T·S
COLORS

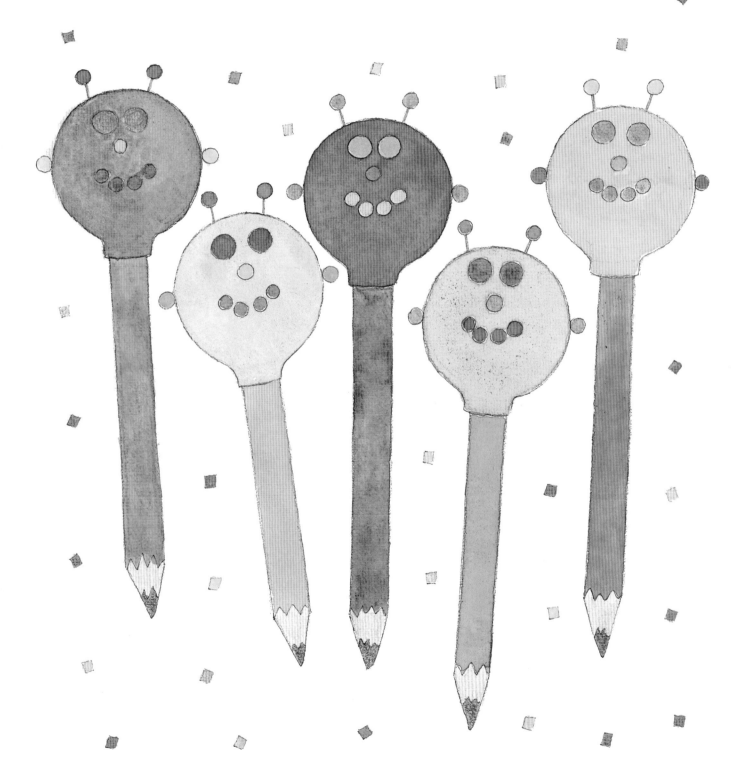

Some apples are red.

apples
strawberries
cranberries
cherries

Red Apple Notepad

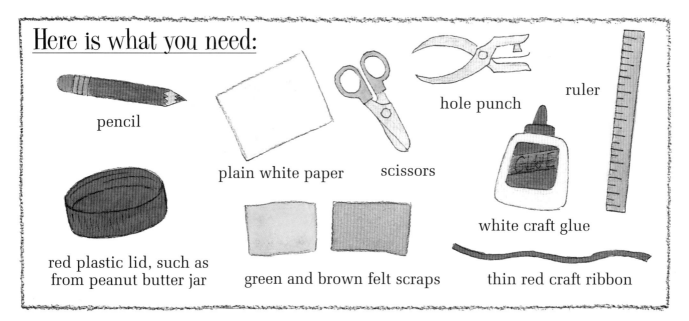

Here is what you need:

pencil

plain white paper

scissors

hole punch

ruler

white craft glue

red plastic lid, such as from peanut butter jar

green and brown felt scraps

thin red craft ribbon

Here is what you do:

1. Use the pencil to trace around the red lid on a piece of the white paper. Cut out the traced circle.

2. Trim the circle around the edges until it fits inside the lid. This will be the pattern that you will use to cut the rest of the paper for the pad.

3. Trace around the pattern on another part of the sheet of white paper. Cut out several stacks of six to eight sheets of paper until you have about fifty sheets of paper.

4. Punch two holes about 1 inch (2.5 cm) apart at the edge of the stack of papers. You will need to do this by punching a few sheets at a time, then using the pencil to mark the location of the holes to punch the next stack of papers.

5. Cut a 6-inch (15-cm) piece of the red ribbon. Stack the paper, lining up the holes, and use the red ribbon to loosely tie the stack together. Tie the ribbon in a bow.

6. Glue the bottom paper of the stack to the inside of the lid to secure it.

7. Cut a brown apple stem and a green leaf from the felt scraps. Turn the lid over so that the pad is on the back and glue the stem and leaf to the top edge of the lid.

This **red apple notepad** is a pretty way to keep notepaper handy.

Make your own big red dog friend.

Big Red Dog Puppet

Here is what you need:

black pipe cleaner

paper fastener

black pom-pom

jingle bell

two wiggle eyes

two red plastic disposable cups

black construction paper scraps

white craft glue

scissors

ruler

Here is what you do:

1. Turn one cup over and poke a small hole in the bottom. This will be the body of the dog.

2. Turn the second cup on one side and poke a hole through the side about halfway down the cup. This cup will form the head for the dog.

3. Push the paper fastener through the inside of the hole in the head cup and then through the hole in the body cup to attach the head to the body. Spread out the arms of the fastener inside the body cup to secure the two cups together.

4. Cut two floppy ears for the dog from the black paper scrap. Glue an ear toward the back of each side of the head.

5. Glue the two wiggle eyes on the top part of the head about halfway down.

6. Give the dog a nose by gluing the black pom-pom to the bottom of the head cup.

7. Cut a 6-inch (15-cm) piece of pipe cleaner to make a collar for the dog. String a jingle bell on the pipe cleaner. Wrap the pipe cleaner collar around the neck of the dog puppet, and wrap the ends around each other to secure the collar with the jingle bell hanging down in front.

To use the dog puppet, place one hand inside the body of the dog and the other hand inside the back of the head to turn it so it can look around. Arf!

9

Pigs are pink.

Pink Plate Piggy Bank

Here is what you need:

pink pipe cleaner

thin pink craft ribbon

pink poster paint and a paintbrush

two large wiggle eyes

large two-hole button

three 9-inch (23-cm) uncoated paper plates

pink paper

white craft glue

scissors

newspaper to work on

ruler

Here is what you do:

1. Cut a 2-inch (5-cm) slit near the edge of one of the paper plates for the money slot.

2. Squeeze a line of glue three quarters of the way around the edge of the eating side of the second plate. Turn the plate so that the edge with no glue is at the top. Set the plate with the slot, eating side down, on the plate with the gluey edge, with the slot touching the edge where there is no glue.

3. Cut a 6-inch (15-cm) piece of the pipe cleaner for a tail. Curl the tail by wrapping it around your finger. Slide one end of the tail in between the glued edges of the front and back of the pig on the right side of the body.

4. Cut a head for the pig from the center of the third paper plate. Glue the head to the left side of the body so that it looks like the pig is sideways.

5. Cut two triangle ears from the scraps of the rim of the paper plate left from cutting out the head. Glue the two ears to the top of the head.

6. Cut four legs for the pig from the scraps. Glue the top ends of two of the legs to the front bottom portion of the pig. Glue the other two legs to the back side of the pig.

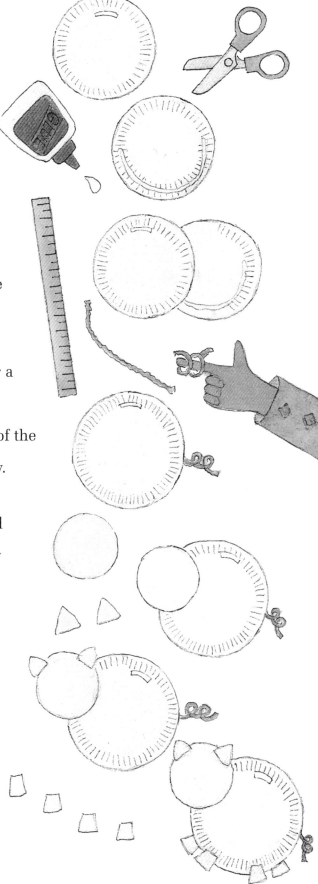

7. Paint the entire pig pink and let the paint dry.

8. Glue the two wiggle eyes on the head. Glue the button below the eyes for the snout.

9. Shape a smile for the pig from a piece of the pink pipe cleaner. Glue the smile in place.

10. Cut small hearts, flowers, or other shapes from the pink paper. Glue the shapes on the pig to decorate it.

11. Punch two small holes through the front and the back of the pig on each side of the unglued opening at the top of the pig. Cut a 2-foot (60-cm) length of pink ribbon. Thread the ribbon through the two holes, then tie the ends together to make a hanger for the pig.

Find a place in your room to hang your piggy bank. Drop your extra coins in the slot of the pig for safekeeping. To get them out easily, just loosen the ribbon at the top and shake the money out of the piggy bank through the opening.

Oink!

Goldfish are orange!

Orange Fish Bath Toy

Here is what you need:

twist top from
soda bottle

small (7-inch/18-cm)
orange balloon

black permanent
marker

Here is what you do:

1. Work the balloon over the cap to cover it. The cap should be in the round part of the balloon to shape the body of the fish, with the neck of the balloon forming the tail.

2. Use the permanent marker to give the fish two eyes on the part of the balloon covering the top edge of the cap.

Make lots of **orange fish** to swim around your bathtub.

Pumpkins are orange.

Five little pumpkins
Sitting on a gate.
The first one said, "I think it's getting late."
The second one said, "There are witches in the air."
The third one said, "I don't care."
The fourth one said, "Let's run and run and run."
The fifth one said, "Isn't Halloween fun?"
Then Whooooo . . . went the wind and
Out went the lights.
And the five little pumpkins rolled out of sight.

—Traditional

Five Orange Pumpkins Puppet

Here is what you need:

brown marker

green pipe cleaner

cardboard egg carton

two rubber bands

scissors

orange poster paint
and a paintbrush

ruler

black construction
paper scraps

white craft glue

newspaper to work on

corrugated cardboard box

Here is what you do:

1. Cut the front strip of six egg cups off the carton. Cut part of the lid off the carton leaving a 1-inch (2.5-cm)-wide strip attached to the egg cups. Cut off one egg cup and the lid portion that is attached to it. You should now have five egg cups for the five pumpkins, with a folding strip along the bottom that will be used to attach the pumpkins to the gate.

2. Paint the strip of pumpkins orange and let the paint dry.

3. Cut facial features for each pumpkin from the black paper scraps. Glue a face on each pumpkin.

4. Cut five 1/2-inch (.12-cm) pieces from the green pipe cleaner for the stems. Glue a stem to the top of each pumpkin.

5. Cut a flap from the corrugated cardboard box to use to make the gate. Trim off one end of the gate so it is only an inch longer than the strip of pumpkins.

6. Use the brown marker to add details to the cardboard gate.

7. Glue the flap at the bottom of the pumpkins to the back of the gate. The pumpkins should look like they are sitting on the gate.

8. Poke a hole in the back of the center pumpkin. Put the remaining piece of pipe cleaner through the hole and twist the two ends together.

9. Put a rubber band around the top and another around the bottom of the gate.

To use the pumpkin puppet slip one hand through the rubber bands at the back of one side of the puppet. Use your other hand to pull on the pipe cleaner to make the pumpkins fold back out of sight.

15

Corn is yellow and yummy!

Yellow Pages Corn Magnet

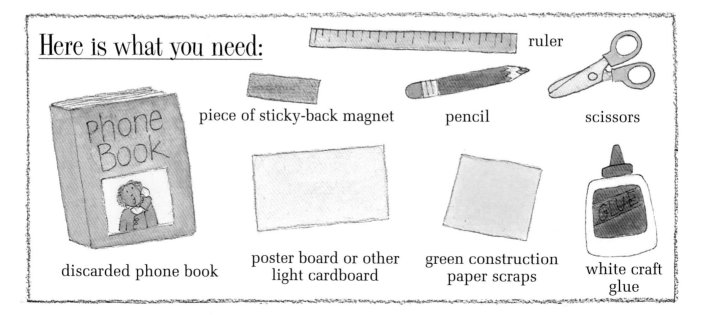

Here is what you need:

ruler

piece of sticky-back magnet

pencil

scissors

discarded phone book

poster board or other light cardboard

green construction paper scraps

white craft glue

Here is what you do:

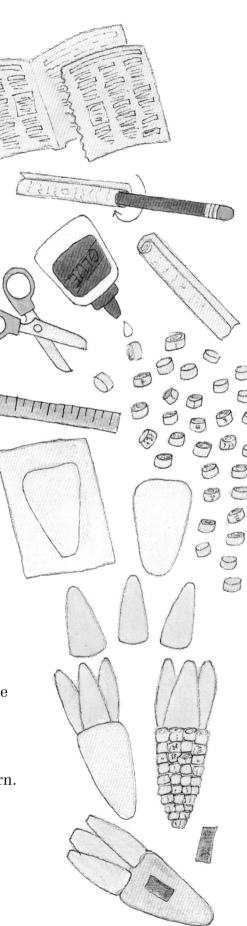

1. Choose a sheet from the yellow pages of the phone book. Tear the sheet out of the phone book.

2. Roll the sheet as tightly as possible into a tube. It is helpful to start by rolling the paper around a pencil then slipping the pencil out before continuing to roll.

3. Secure the edge of the rolled paper with glue.

4. Cut the roll of paper into 1/4-inch (0.5-cm)-long rolls to use as the corn kernels.

5. Use the pencil to draw a 3-inch (8-cm)-long ear of corn on the cardboard. Cut out the corn shape.

6. Cut some 3-inch (8-cm) strips from the green paper. Glue the strips to the back of the wide end of the ear of corn so that they stick up from the corn like peeled-back husks.

7. Glue the rings cut from the rolled yellow page all over the corn to look like the kernels.

8. Press a piece of sticky-back magnet on the back of the corn.

Use the magnet to hold your "good work" on the refrigerator for everyone to see. You'll probably need more than one!

Some caterpillars are yellow, and they all are creepy-crawly.

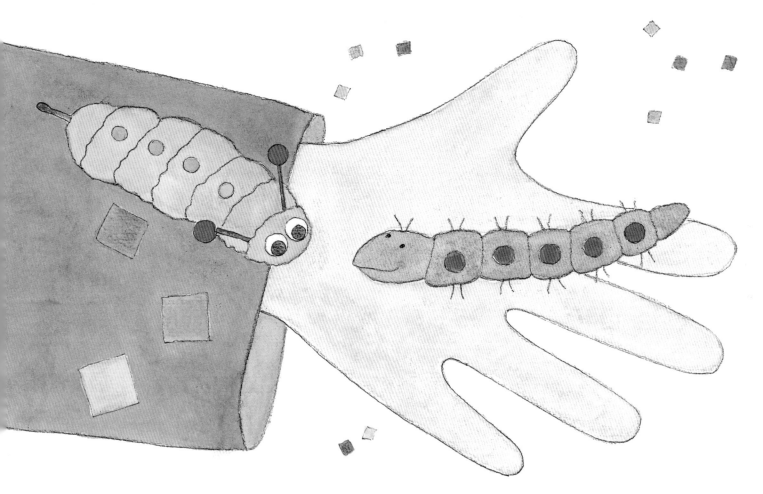

Yellow Caterpillar Cuff Pin

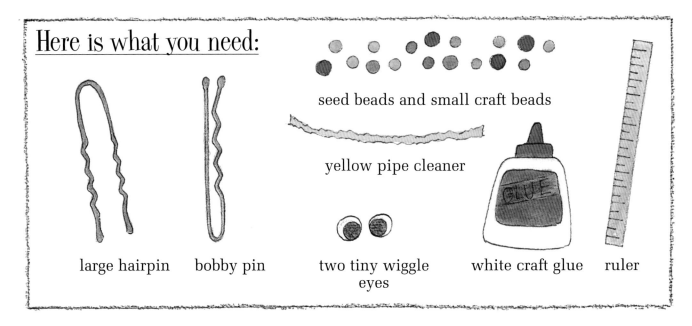

Here is what you need:

seed beads and small craft beads

yellow pipe cleaner

two tiny wiggle eyes

white craft glue

large hairpin

bobby pin

ruler

GLUE

Here is what you do:

1. Fold up a 1/2-inch (1.25-cm) piece of each end of the hairpin to form antennas for the caterpillar.

2. Wrap the remainder of the hairpin with the yellow pipe cleaner to make the body, leaving a 1-inch (2.5-cm)-long end sticking up.

3. Slide the shorter prong of the bobby pin into the wrapped pipe cleaner. Continue wrapping the body so that the bobby pin is attached to the bottom of the caterpillar. The bobby pin will be used to attach the caterpillar to your cuff.

4. Glue two wiggle eyes to the front of the caterpillar.

5. Decorate the caterpillar by gluing a bead to the tip of each antenna and on the back of the caterpillar.

To wear the caterpillar, slip the bobby pin over the end of a cuff or collar.

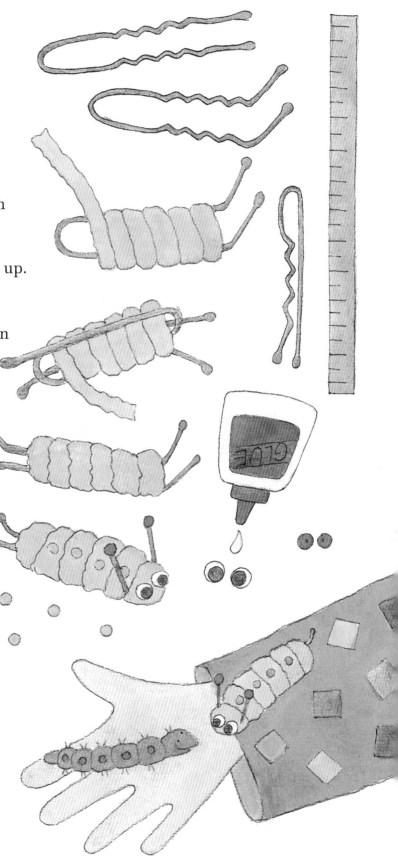

Some frogs are green.

Green Frog Zipper Pull

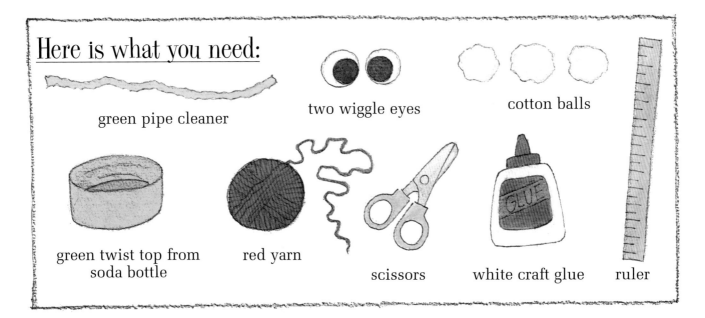

Here is what you need:

green pipe cleaner

two wiggle eyes

cotton balls

green twist top from soda bottle

red yarn

scissors

white craft glue

ruler

Here is what you do:

1. Cut four 2-inch (5-cm) pieces of pipe cleaner for the arms and legs of the frog.

2. Cover the inside of the cap with glue.

3. Place the ends of two pieces of pipe cleaner in the glue in the cap so that they hang down for the legs.

4. Place the ends of the other two pieces of pipe cleaner in the glue so that they stick out on each side of the cap for the arms.

5. Cover the glue in the cap with a cotton ball to fill it.

6. Trim the ends of the arms so that they are slightly shorter than the legs.

7. Bend the end of each leg forward to form feet.

8. Glue the two wiggle eyes to the top of the cap so that they are sticking up slightly over the edge like bulging frog eyes.

9. Cut a 3/4-inch (2-cm) piece of red yarn. Glue the yarn across the cap under the eyes for a mouth.

Slip the end of one of the frog arms through the hole in the zipper of a backpack or jacket. Fold the pipe cleaner end down so that the frog looks like it is hanging on to the zipper. Ribbet!

Monsters are green?

Green Monster Gift Bag

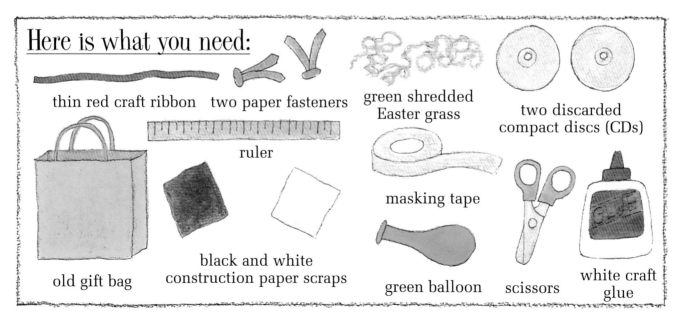

Here is what you need:

thin red craft ribbon   two paper fasteners

green shredded Easter grass

two discarded compact discs (CDs)

ruler

masking tape

old gift bag

black and white construction paper scraps

green balloon   scissors   white craft glue

Here is what you do:

1. Cover one side of the gift bag with glue, then press the shredded grass over the glue to cover the bag.

2. Cut two 2-inch (5-cm) circles from the black paper for the pupils for the eyes.

3. Push a paper fastener through the center of each pupil, then through the hole in one of the CDs, then through the top portion of the grass-covered bag to attach the two eyes to the face.

4. Cut a 5-inch (13-cm) length of the red ribbon for the mouth. Glue the ribbon mouth across the bottom part of the face.

5. Cut two pointed teeth from the white paper scraps. Glue the two teeth to the mouth.

6. Poke a hole through the center of the bag where the nose should be.

7. Inflate the green balloon to about 4 inches (10 cm) across and knot it. Insert the knot through the hole in the bag so that the balloon becomes the nose for the monster face. Secure the knot of the balloon inside the bag using masking tape.

This bag not only makes a creative gift container, but it can also be used for storing important stuff or as a trick or treat bag. Grrr . . . !

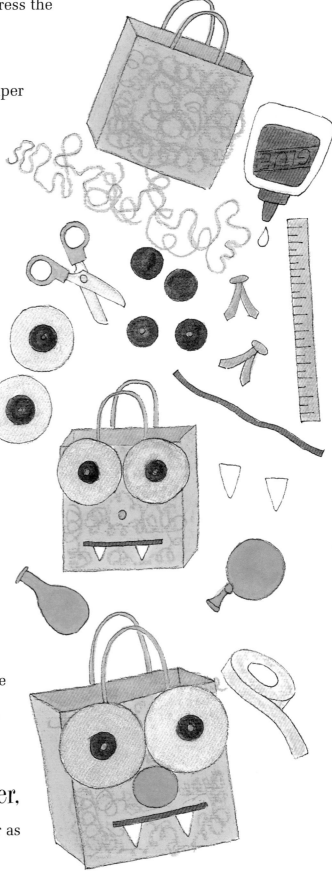

23

Bluebirds are blue, of course!

"If happy little bluebirds fly over the rainbow,
why, oh, why can't I?"

—Dorothy, in *The Wizard of Oz*

Bluebirds over the Rainbow Magnet

Here is what you need:

black pen

sticky-back magnet

ruler

scissors

white craft glue

clear packing tape

discarded jigsaw puzzle
picturing blue sky or water

red, orange, yellow, green, blue, and purple pipe cleaners

Here is what you do:

1. Find six blue puzzle pieces with a round knob on top and "arms" on each side.

2. Trim each piece so that it has a pointed tail at one end, a knob head at the other, and one "wing" on each side to look like a bird in flight.

3. Use the pen to give each "bird" two eyes and a beak on the knob head.

4. Cut a 5-inch (13-cm) piece of pipe cleaner in each of the rainbow colors listed.

5. You will need to do the next part on a nonstick surface like a kitchen counter. Unroll a 6-inch (15-cm) piece of tape and fold the end back to stick it to the counter. Do not cut the tape from the roll yet. Set the roll of tape on the counter to hold down the other end of the strip.

6. Stick the pipe cleaners on the tape to make a part of a rainbow. Start with the red one on top, then orange, yellow, green, blue, and purple.

7. Cut the tape from the roll. Trim off all tape that is not covered by the pipe cleaners.

8. Gently shape the rainbow into an arch. You will need to trim the ends again to make them even.

9. Glue the bluebirds to the front of the rainbow to look like they are flying over it.

10. Attach two or three pieces of sticky-back magnet to the back of the rainbow.

Some flowers are blue.

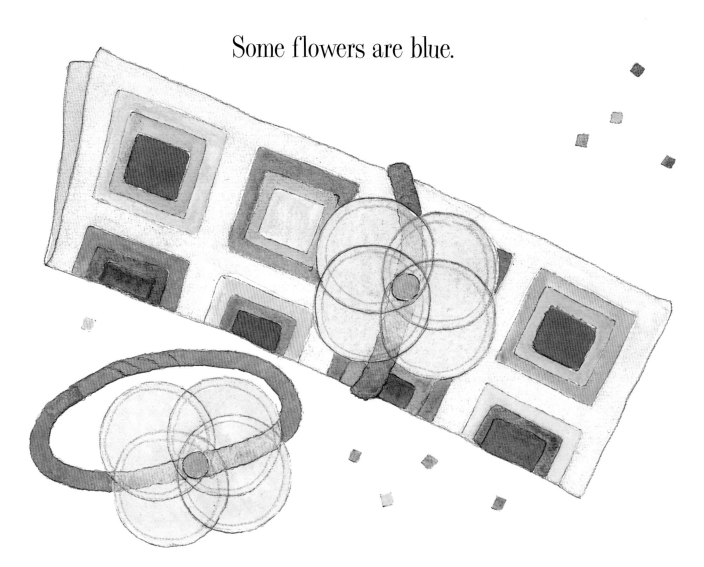

Blue Flower Napkin Ring

Here is what you need for each napkin ring:

blue pipe cleaner

paper fasteners

four twist tops from
Coca-Cola® bottles

scissors

tiny hole punch

ruler

Here is what you do:

1. Pry the light blue lining out of each of the four tops.

2. Punch a tiny hole through the edge of each blue liner.

3. Push the paper fastener through the hole in each of the four liners. Arrange the four circle liners to look like the petals of a flower.

4. Cut a 6-inch (15-cm) piece of the blue pipe cleaner.

5. Attach the flower to the middle of the pipe cleaner by wrapping the arms of the paper fastener around it.

6. Pull the ends of the pipe cleaner around to form a 2-inch (5-cm) circle. Secure the circle by wrapping the ends of the pipe cleaner around itself.

You might want to save enough caps to make a set of these napkin rings and give them as a gift. How pretty!

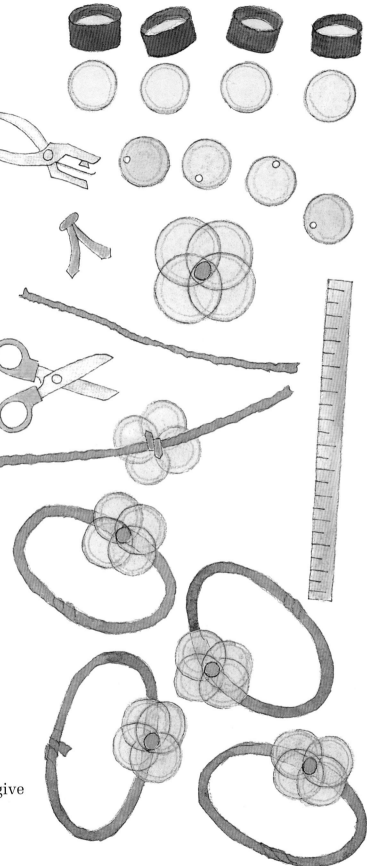

Some grapes are purple.

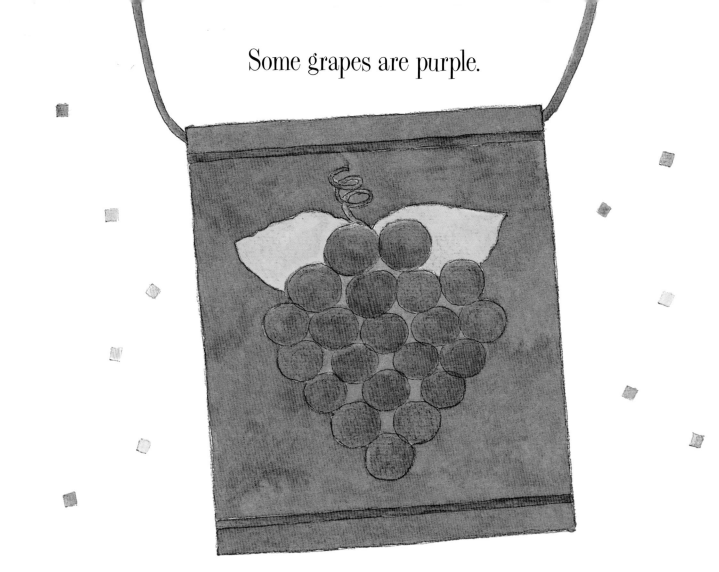

Purple Grapes Wall Hanging

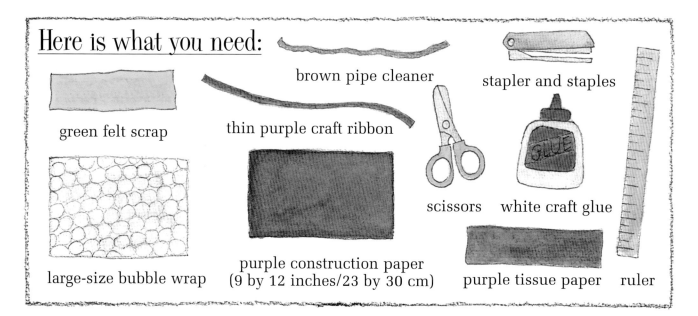

Here is what you need:

brown pipe cleaner

stapler and staples

green felt scrap

thin purple craft ribbon

scissors   white craft glue

large-size bubble wrap

purple construction paper
(9 by 12 inches/23 by 30 cm)

purple tissue paper   ruler

Here is what you do:

1. Cut a triangle shape from the bubble wrap that has one bubble at the point, then two, and so on up to seven bubbles across.

2. Cut one bubble off each side of the top two rows so that the triangle shape tapers in.

3. Cut several 2- to 3-inch (5- to 8-cm) squares of purple tissue paper.

4. Cut a slit in the back of each bubble and fill all of them with crumpled purple tissue.

5. Gather the tops of the bubble-wrap grapes together to give the bunch a curved three-dimensional look. Secure the bunch with staples.

6. Fold a scrap of green felt. Cut a leaf shape from the felt. Open the cut shape so that you have two leaves. Gather the center of the two leaves and secure with a stapler to give them a three-dimensional look.

7. Wrap a 6-inch (15-cm) piece of the brown pipe cleaner around your finger to make a vine and staple it to the back of the leaves. Staple the leaves and vine to the back of the top of the bunch of grapes.

8. Fold down one of the 9-inch (23-cm) sides of the sheet of purple paper.

9. Cut a 2-foot (60-cm) length of ribbon and center it under the fold. Secure with staples.

10. Tie the ends of the ribbon to make a hanger.

You might want to add purple trims or ribbon to the edges of the hanging to decorate it further.

Make your own purple purse.

Purple Purse

Here is what you need:

paintbrush

tiny hole punch

three paper fasteners

scissors

music button
from craft store

aluminum foil

purple tissue paper

white craft glue

DAILY NEWS

newspaper to
work on

ruler

Here is what you do:

1. Tear off a square of aluminum foil to make the purse. Tear off a 4-inch (10-cm)-wide strip for the handle.

2. Use the paintbrush to cover both pieces of foil with glue.

3. Cover both glued foil pieces with a sheet of purple tissue paper. The tissue does not have to be an exact fit.

4. When the glue has dried, trim the edges of the tissue to the edge of the foil.

5. Fold up the bottom third of the square to shape a purse with the purple tissue on the outside.

6. Fold in the edges of the purse on each side.

7. Fold in corners of the purse flap to round them.

8. Fold in the edges of the strip of foil to make a handle for the purse.

9. Punch a hole in each end of the handle.

10. Punch a hole in each side of the purse at the top where the front and back overlap.

11. Use a paper fastener to attach an end of the handle to each side of the purse through the holes.

12. Punch a hole in the center of the flap of the purse. Put a paper fastener through the hole and bend the back prongs to secure it to look like a clasp.

If you are lucky enough to have a music button, stick in inside the purse. Then you can open the purse and press the button to hear music. Remember not to play music during class!

31

These two little blackbirds are perfect
to use with this nursery rhyme.

Two little blackbirds
sitting on a hill.
One named Jack,
the other named Jill.
Fly away, Jack!
Fly away, Jill!
Come back, Jack!
Come back, Jill!

—Traditional

Two Little Blackbird

Finger Puppets

Here is what you need:

four seed beads

scissors

thin craft ribbon

two discarded black
marker caps

black and yellow felt scraps

white craft glue   ruler

Here is what you do:

1. Fold the black felt in half and cut a 2-inch (5-cm) wing on the fold. Open the folded wing so that you have two wings attached at the center. Make a set of wings for each blackbird.

2. Glue the center of the wings to the middle of the side of the cap for each bird.

3. The opening of the cap will be the bottom of the blackbird. Cut two tiny triangle beaks from the yellow felt. Glue a beak to the top portion of each blackbird between the wings.

4. Glue on two seed beads above each beak for the eyes.

5. Cut two 3-inch (8-cm) pieces of ribbon. Tie a knot in each piece. Trim and glue the ends to make two tiny bows.

6. Glue one bow at the neck of the bird for a bow tie for "Jack." Glue the other bow to one side of the top of the head of the second bird for a hair bow for "Jill."

Put a blackbird on a finger of each hand. Try saying the rhyme and using the blackbird finger puppets to act it out. When the birds fly away, hide them behind you.

My favorite kind of top hat is a magic hat!

Black Magic Top Hat Necklace

Here is what you need:

two small wiggle eyes

cotton swab

gold sticker stars

black yarn

pink seed bead

cotton balls

black film canister

black construction paper scrap

scissors

white craft glue

ruler

Here is what you do:

1. Cut a 2-inch (5-cm) circle from the black construction paper.

2. Cut an X-shaped slit in the center of the circle.

3. Rub glue around the rim and entire inside of the film canister.

4. Place the black circle on the rim of the canister. Press the cut center of the circle to open the circle and stick the sides to the inside of the film canister.

5. Put enough cotton balls in the canister to fill it to about three-quarters full. The cotton will be the rabbit.

6. Cut off the ends of the cotton swab for ears.

7. Glue the stick end of the two ears, side by side, sticking up from the cotton balls.

8. Glue the two wiggle eyes in front of the ears.

9. Glue the pink seed bead in front of the eyes for a nose.

10. Decorate the outside of the hat with gold sticker stars.

11. Cut a 3-foot (90-cm) length of yarn. Tie the yarn around the hat under the brim. Tie the ends of the yarn together to make the necklace.

Is that a **rabbit** in your hat?

35

Find some gray stones and use them to
make a family of little gray mice.

Gray Stone Mouse

Here is what you need:

two black seed beads

pink felt scrap

hole punch

1- to 2-inch (2- to 5-cm)
gray stone

black or brown
embroidery floss

scissors

white craft
glue

ruler

Here is what you do:

1. Use the hole punch to punch two circle ears from the pink felt.

2. Glue the ears to the top of one end of the stone.

3. Glue the seed beads under the ears for eyes for the mouse.

4. Knot a 2-inch (5-cm) piece of the embroidery floss. Trim the ends and spread the threads to make whiskers for the mouse. Glue on the whiskers under the eyes.

5. Cut a 3-inch (8-cm) piece of embroidery floss. Glue the piece to the back of the mouse for a tail.

6. Cut a small piece of felt to glue on the bottom of the mouse to prevent the stone from scratching a table surface.

Make the mouse some brothers and sisters.

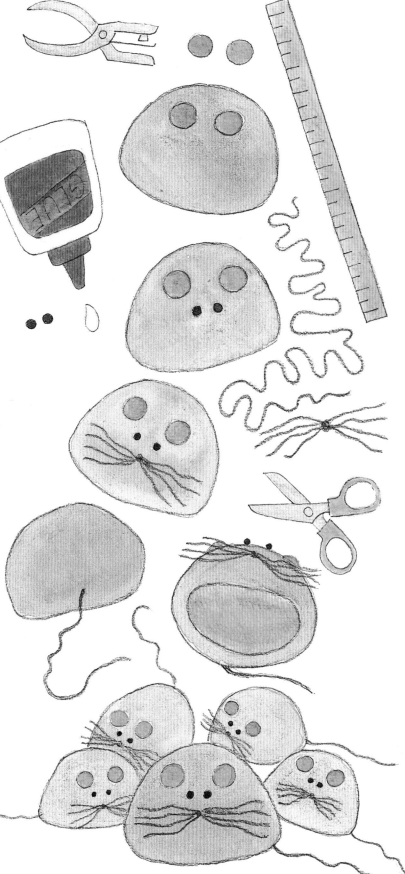

Turn brown paper bags into brown dog
disguises for you and your doll friend.

Brown Bag Dog Disguise

Here is what you need:

black marker

scissors

white craft glue

brown grocery bag

brown lunch bag

black construction paper

ruler

Here is what you do:

1. Cut most of the neck off the balloon.

2. Pull the balloon over the Styrofoam ball to cover it.

3. Use the point of the pencil to poke a small hole in the Styrofoam ball through the opening of the balloon. Turn over the pencil and push the ball onto the eraser end of the pencil.

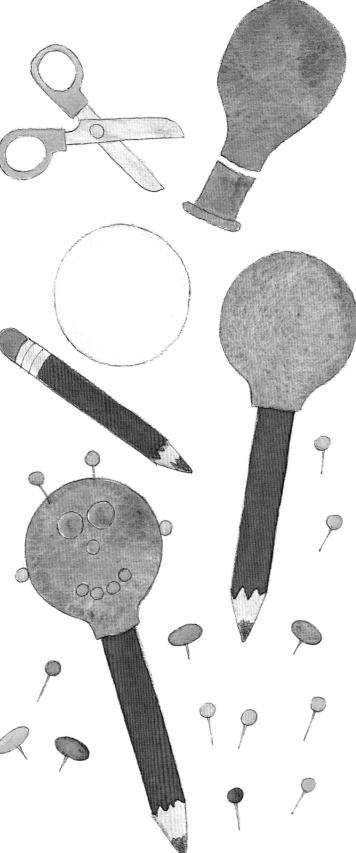

4. Use the thumbtacks and map pins to create a face for the alien. If a map pin hits the pencil, just wiggle it around until the pin angles around the pencil.

Alien pencil tops make a great party favor.

Make a whole family of color friends.

Chatty Color Family Puppets

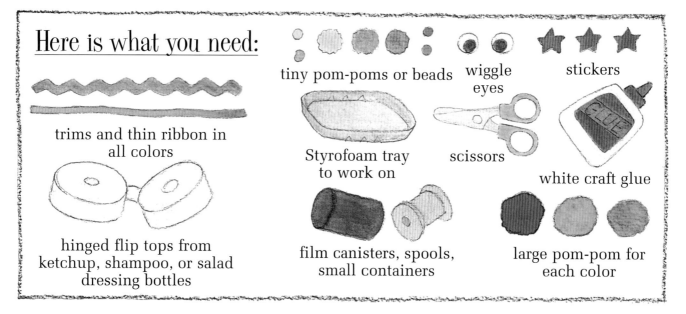

Here is what you need:

trims and thin ribbon in all colors

hinged flip tops from ketchup, shampoo, or salad dressing bottles

tiny pom-poms or beads

Styrofoam tray to work on

film canisters, spools, small containers

wiggle eyes

scissors

stickers

white craft glue

large pom-pom for each color

Here is what you do:

1. For each color friend choose a large pom-pom for the hair. This will determine the color name of each friend. Turn over the cap and glue the pom-pom hair in the open end.

2. The hinged top of the cap will now become the bottom jaw of the puppet. Glue two wiggle eyes and a tiny pom-pom or bead nose on the front of the cap above the mouth opening.

3. Glue the bottom of the head to the bottom of a film canister or other small container or base such as a spool. Make sure that the cap will still open and shut to "talk." With some caps you will have to slide the cap back slightly so that the hinge is over the edge of the container to avoid obstruction.

4. Decorate the body of each puppet with trims or stickers in the color of the hair.

If the puppets have open containers for the body, you might want to pack the openings lightly with fiberfill and use them as finger puppets.

45

Fill the air in your room with colorful birds.

Color Birds Stabile

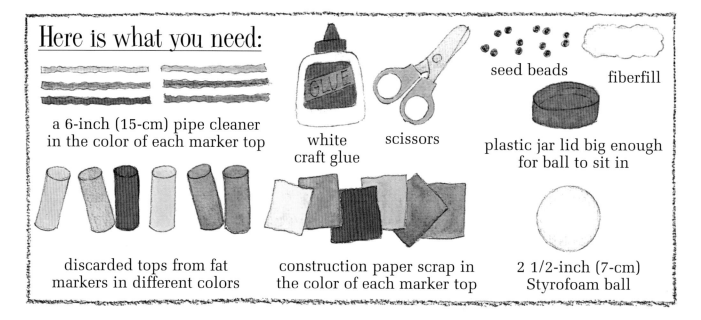

Here is what you need:

a 6-inch (15-cm) pipe cleaner in the color of each marker top

white craft glue

scissors

seed beads

fiberfill

plastic jar lid big enough for ball to sit in

discarded tops from fat markers in different colors

construction paper scrap in the color of each marker top

2 1/2-inch (7-cm) Styrofoam ball

Here is what you do:

1. Cut across one side of the Styrofoam ball to flatten it.

2. Glue the flat side of the ball into the plastic lid to make a base for the stabile.

3. Stick a pipe cleaner into the Styrofoam ball to match each color bird you are making.

4. Turn each marker cap into a bird. To do this, fold in half a paper scrap that is the same color as the cap. Cut a wing on the fold. Unfold the wing so that you have two wings that are attached at the center.

5. Glue the wings on the side of the cap.

6. Cut a tiny triangle beak from construction paper.

7. Glue the beak to the top of the marker cap.

8. Glue two seed beads above the beak for eyes.

9. Slip the open end of the bird over the matching color pipe cleaner.

10. Spread glue over the Styrofoam ball. Cover the gluey ball with fiberfill to look like a cloud.

You may need to move some of the pipe cleaners and arrange the angles of the birds to make the stabile balance.

47

About the Author and Artist

Thirty years as a teacher and director of nursery school programs have given Kathy Ross extensive experience in guiding young children through craft projects. Among the more than forty craft books she has written are CRAFTS FOR ALL SEASONS, MAKE YOURSELF A MONSTER, THE BEST BIRTHDAY PARTIES EVER, THE BEST CHRISTMAS CRAFTS EVER, and THE STORYTIME CRAFT BOOK. She is also the author of the popular *Holiday Crafts for Kids* series, and the *Crafts for Kids Who Are Wild About . . .* series.

Learn more about Kathy and download new crafts by visiting kathyross.com

Jan Barger, originally from Little Rock, Arkansas, now lives in Plumpton, East Sussex, England, with her husband and their cocker spaniel, Tosca. As well as writing and illustrating children's books, she designs greeting cards, sings with the Brighton Festival Chorus, and plays piccolo with the Sinfonia of Arun.

Kathy and Jan together have created the other books in this series: KATHY ROSS CRAFTS LETTER SHAPES; KATHY ROSS CRAFTS LETTER SOUNDS; KATHY ROSS CRAFTS TRIANGLES, RECTANGLES, CIRCLES, AND SQUARES; and KATHY ROSS CRAFTS NUMBERS.